The Big Snowball

By Paul Shipton

Illustrated by Fabiano Fiorin

Activities by Hannah Fish

Contents

Hello!
My name is Ben.
Hello!
My name is Rosie.
This is
Grandpa.
This is Grandpa's
van. It's fantastic!

Ben
Rosie's brother
Rosie
Ben's sister
Grandpa
Clunk
Grandpa's robot
Alice
Rosie's friend
Now let's read this story,
The Big Snowball.

'Where are we going today, Grandpa?' asks Ben.

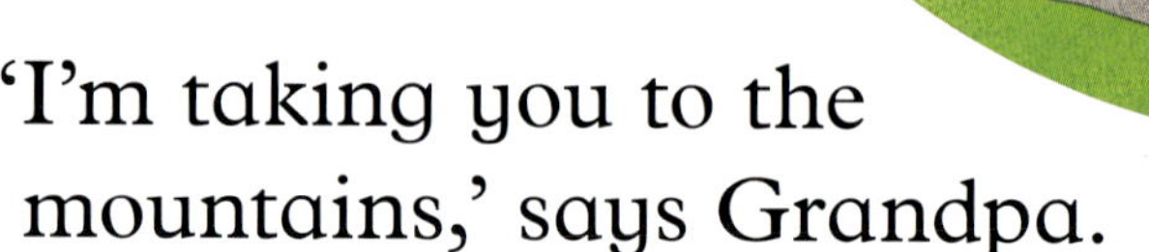

'I'm taking you to the mountains,' says Grandpa.

Alice is happy. 'I love playing in the snow!' she says.

But when the van stops, the children can't see any snow.

'It's too hot for snow in these mountains,' says Grandpa.

'We can go for a nice, long walk,' says Grandpa. 'Come on!'

They start to walk on a little path in the mountains.

The mountains are beautiful, but soon the children are hot and thirsty.

They meet a family on the path.

'Hello,' says the father. 'We're looking for the lake. Can you help?'

Grandpa points. 'The lake is a long way from here,' he says.

The family are not happy to hear that. They are hot, tired, and thirsty.

Grandpa stops and thinks. 'Maybe it
IS too hot here today,' he says.

'It's the hottest summer here ever!' says
Clunk.

Grandpa starts to go to the van again.
'I have a new idea!' he says. 'Let's go to
some COLDER mountains!'

Go to page 22 for activities.

Soon the van is in a new place.

'That's better!' says Alice. 'These mountains are very snowy!'

The children put on big coats and hats. Then they run to play in the snow.

'Don't go close to the edge, please,' says Grandpa. 'We are very high here.'

Rosie makes a snowball. She rolls it, and it gets bigger and bigger.

'Let's make a snowman!' she says. 'This can be the head!'

'That's a good idea,' says Ben. 'I can make a very big snowball for the snowman's body.'

Go to page 24 for activities.

Ben's snowball gets bigger and bigger.

'Ben!' shouts Rosie. 'You're getting close to the edge.'

Ben stops, but the big snowball doesn't stop. It starts to roll down the mountain.

Ben watches it. 'Oh no!' he says.

The big snowball is fast.
It picks up more and more
snow, and it gets bigger and bigger.

Rosie is scared. 'Look,' she says.
'There's a little house at the bottom
of the mountain.'

'I can stop that snowball,' says Clunk.
'I'm very fast when I ski. Watch!'

→ Go to page 26 for activities.

Clunk skis down the mountain after the big snowball.

The snowball is fast, but Clunk is faster!

When he is in the right place, he stops and turns. But now the big snowball is bigger than Clunk. It's bigger than a car!

'Oh dear,' says the little robot.

The big snowball hits Clunk. Now it is rolling down the mountain with Clunk in it!

'Help!' shouts Clunk. He can't stop the snowball. It picks up more snow – now the snowball is bigger than a bus!

At the top of the mountain, the children run to the van.

'Quick, Grandpa!' says Rosie. 'Let's help Clunk!'

Grandpa starts the van and drives down the mountain. The big snowball is very fast but Grandpa's fantastic van is a lot faster! It flies over the snow.

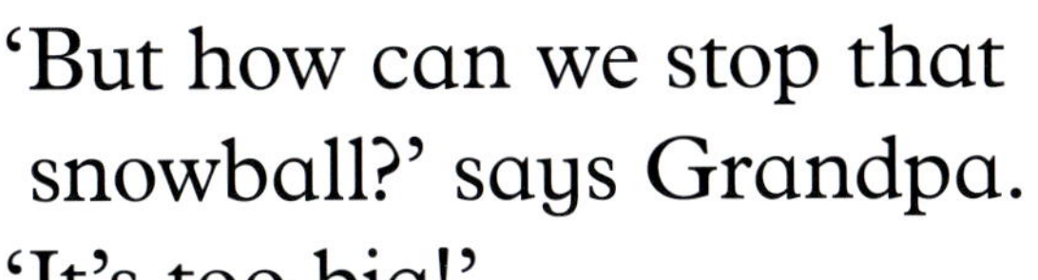

'But how can we stop that snowball?' says Grandpa. 'It's too big!'

'I have an idea,' says Alice. 'You have to fly the van in front of the snowball. Quick!'

'OK,' says Grandpa.

Soon the van is in front of the big snowball. But the snowball is very close to the little house …

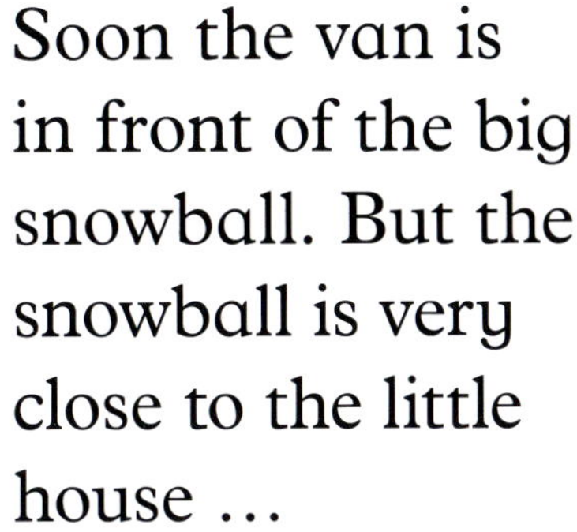

Go to page 30 for activities.

'Three, two, one … NOW!' says Alice.

Grandpa hits the computer screen with his finger.

'Then there are lights in front of the van and the van flies into them …

When the van flies out of the lights,
it's in the hot, sunny mountains again.

Ben looks behind the van. 'Look!
The big snowball's here, too!' he says.

'But it isn't stopping,' says Rosie.

'That's OK,' says Alice. 'Watch it …'

→ Go to page 32 for activities.

Very soon the big snowball can't roll because it starts to melt.

'It's too hot here for a snowball!' says Alice.

Soon Clunk can move again.

'Thank you!' he says, and he jumps up.

The family in the mountains
run to the big snowball.

'This is fantastic!' says the girl.

'We can make snowballs!' says the boy.

But soon the snowball is a pool of water.

'You can't make snowballs,' says Ben.
'But you can have a nice, cold drink!'

Go to page 34 for activities.

1 Write the words.

1 <u>m o u n t a i n</u>

2 _ _ _ _ _ _

3 _ _ _ _ _

4 _ _ _ _ _

5 _ _ _ _ _

2 Circle the correct words.

1 Grandpa takes the children **at** / **to** the mountains.

2 Alice loves playing **for** / **in** the snow.

3 The children **can't** / **aren't** see any snow.

4 The mountains are **too** / **to** hot for snow.

5 They walk on **an** / **a** little path in the mountains.

6 Soon the children **are** / **is** hot and thirsty.

3 **Look at the picture on page 5.
Answer the questions.**

1 Where are Grandpa and
the children?   in the _mountains_

2 Who is next to Rosie?   _______________

3 Is Clunk with Grandpa and
the children?   _______________

4 What color are Alice's shoes?   _______________

5 Is it hot here?   _______________

6 Can you see any animals?   _______________

4 **Order the words.**

1 and the / children / the mountains. /
Grandpa / go to

Grandpa and the children go to the
mountains.

2 go for / walk. / a / They / nice, long

____

3 and thirsty. / Soon / children / hot / are / the

____

Talk **Do you like to go for a walk?
Where do you go? Talk to a friend.**

 **Activities** for pages 6–7

1 Put a tick (✓) or a cross (✗) in the box.

 **1** This is a family.  ✗

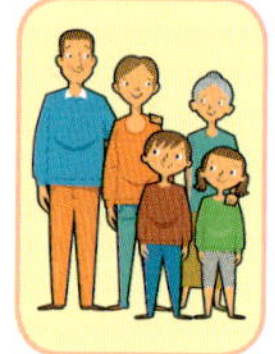 **2** This is the summer. ☐

 **3** This is tired. ☐

 **4** This is point.  ☐

 **5** This is a lake. ☐

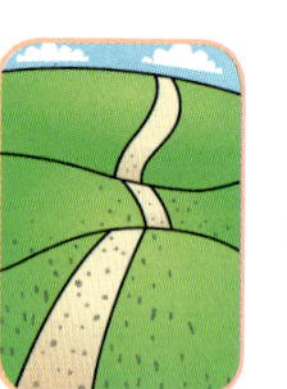 **6** This is an idea.  ☐

Talk **Do you like the mountains? Do you like hot mountains or cold, snowy mountains? Talk to a friend.**

2 Find the words to complete the chart.

new	newer	newest
	thirstier	thirstiest
cold		coldest
	happier	happiest
	longer	longest
hot	hotter	

3 Choose and write the correct words.

Grandpa and the [1] __children__ meet a family. The family are looking for a [2] __________, but it is a long way. The family are [3] __________, tired, and thirsty. Then [4] __________ has an idea. He says, 'Let's go to some COLDER mountains!'

Grandpa

~~children~~

Alice

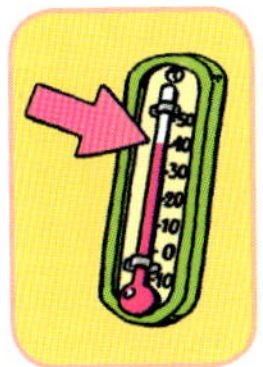
hot

lake

 Activities for pages 8–9

1 Write the words.

1 t a h

hat

2 g e d e

3 l n w l a o b s

4 a o t c

5 w m o s n a n

6 g h i h

2 Match.

1 The van takes them • • in the snow.

2 The children play • • snowman's body.

3 Rosie makes a • • to snowy mountains.

4 Ben makes the • • big snowball.

Talk Can you make a snowman? Talk to a friend.

3 Choose and write the correct words.

Grandpa and [1] _____the_____ children are
[2] _____________ in the mountains. The children put
on coats and hats and run [3] _____________ in the
snow. Rosie makes a snowball. The snowball is
a snowman's [4] _____________ . Ben makes
[5] _____________ big snowball for the snowman's
body.

1 ~~the~~ some a

2 higher highest high

3 playing to play play

4 head hand hat

5 a an that

4 Look at pages 8 and 9 and complete the
sentences. You can use 1, 2, or 3 words.

1 Soon the van is _____in a new_____ place.

2 They are very _____________ in the
mountains.

3 Grandpa says, 'Don't _____________ the
edge, please.'

4 Rosie wants to _____________ snowman.

1 Look at the picture on page 11. Write *yes* or *no*.

1 The snowball is rolling down the mountain. *yes*

2 The children are watching the snowball. ______

3 The snowball is at the bottom of the mountain. ______

4 There is a house at the top of the mountain. ______

5 There are some trees on the mountain. ______

6 Clunk is wearing skis. ______

7 The mountain is very snowy. ______

2 Who says this? Write the names.

1 'I can stop that snowball.' *Clunk*

2 'Ben! You're getting close to the edge.' ______

3 'There's a little house at the bottom of the mountain.' ______

4 'Oh no!' ______

5 'I'm very fast when I ski. Watch!' ______

3 **Choose and write the correct words.**

Ben's snowball gets bigger and bigger. Ben gets
[1] ____________ to the edge of the mountain, and
his snowball starts to [2] ____________ down the
mountain! Rosie is [3] ____________. There is a little
house at the [4] ____________ of the mountain. But
Clunk can stop the snowball. He can [5] ____________,
and he is very fast! The children watch Clunk.

ski

fast

house

scared

close

bottom

down

roll

Talk **Can Clunk get the snowball?
Tell a friend your ideas.**

 **Activities** for pages 12–13

1 Choose and write the correct words.

a robot   a place   ~~a car~~   a bus

1 Lots of people have one of these.
   They drive it when they want to
   go somewhere.   _a car_

2 This can look like a person,
   but is made of metal.   ___________

3 Lots of people can go on this
   when they want to go somewhere.
   It is like a car, but much bigger.   ___________

2 Complete the sentences.

turns   picks   ~~skis~~   hits

1 Clunk ____skis____ after the big snowball.

2 At the right place, Clunk stops and ___________.

3 The big snowball ___________ Clunk.

4 The snowball ___________ up more snow.

3 **Circle the mistakes. Then write the correct words.**

1 Clunk (runs) down the mountain
after the snowball.   _____skis_____

2 Clunk is slower than the snowball. _________

3 At the right place, Clunk stops
and shouts.   _________

4 Now the snowball is smaller
than a car.   _________

5 The snowball hits Clunk and
rolls up the mountain.   _________

6 Clunk can stop the snowball.   _________

4 **Look at the picture on page 13. Write *yes* or *no*.**

1 The snowball is very big.   _______

2 Clunk is in the snowball.   _______

3 There is a cat in the snowball, too. _______

4 Clunk is happy.   _______

5 The snowball is rolling down
the mountain.   _______

Talk **What happens to Clunk and the snowball? Tell a friend your ideas.**

Activities for pages 14–15

1 Write the words.

1 o p t

top

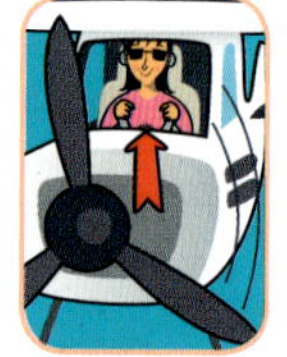

2 l y f

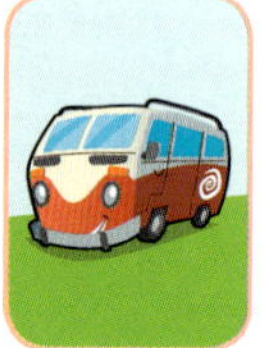

3 n a v

2 Circle the correct answers.

1 Where do the children run?

to the snowball   to Clunk   (to the van)

2 Which is faster?

the snowball   Grandpa's van

3 Who has an idea?

Alice   Rosie   Ben

4 Where does Grandpa have to fly the van?

to the top of the mountain
in front of the snowball

3 Choose the best answers.

1 Grandpa: But how can we stop the snowball?
  Alice: **a** I have an idea!   **b** I get an idea!
              c I am an idea!

2 Grandpa: Oh good. What is your idea?
  Alice: **a** You have for fly the van.
              b You have fly the van.
              c You have to fly the van.

3 Grandpa: Where to?
  Alice: **a** In front of the snowball.
              b In front the snowball.
              c Front of the snowball.

4 Grandpa: Do you want me to do it now?
  Alice: **a** Yes, the snowball's close to the house.
              b Yes, the snowball close to the house.
              c Yes, the snowballs close to the house.

4 Match.

1 The children •   • over the snow.

2 Grandpa drives •   • run to the van.

3 The van flies •   • down the mountain.

 Activities for pages 16–17

1 Put a tick (✓) or a cross (✗) in the box.

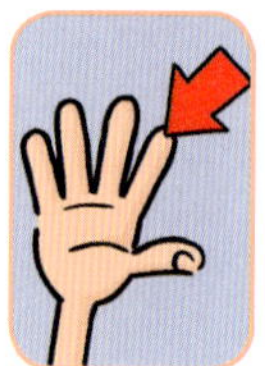

1 This is a finger. ☐

2 This is a light. ☐

3 This is in front of. ☐

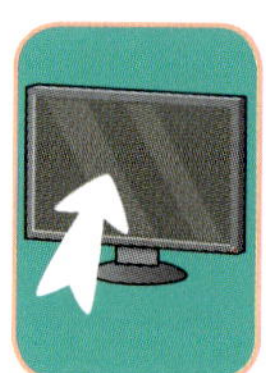

4 This is a screen. ☐

2 Order the words.

1 hits / computer / Grandpa / screen. / the

____

2 lights / the van. / There / in front of / are

____

3 is in / hot / The / mountains again. / van / the

____

4 too! / snowball / there, / is / The

____

3 Choose and write the correct words.

Grandpa hits the [1] ___________ screen, and there are lights in front of the [2] ___________. The van flies into the lights, and is in the [3] ___________ mountains again. [4] ___________ looks behind the van. The [5] ___________ is there, too. The children watch the snowball.

Clunk

computer

van

snowman

snowball

Ben

hot

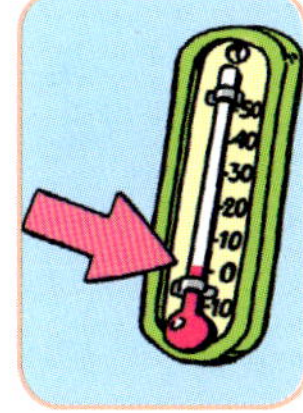

cold

4 Now tick (✓) the best name for pages 16 and 17.

Back in the cold mountains ☐

Back in the high mountains ☐

Back in the hot mountains ☐

1 Write the words.

1 __ __ __ __

2 __ __ __ __ __

3 __ __ __ __

4 __ __ __ __

2 Look at page 18 and complete the sentences. You can use 1, 2, or 3 words.

1 The big snowball _________________ melt.

2 Now the big _________________ can't roll.

3 It's _________________ for a snowball.

4 Now Clunk can _________________ again.

5 Clunk _________________ up.

3 Circle the correct words.

1 It is **too** / **so** hot for a snowball.

2 The big snowball starts **for** / **to** melt.

3 The family **of** / **in** the mountains are there.

4 They **run** / **running** to the big snowball.

5 The boy wants **making** / **to make** snowballs.

6 But soon the snowball is **an** / **a** pool of water.

7 Now the family can **having** / **have** a nice, cold drink!

4 Who says this? Write the names.

1 'We can make snowballs!' ___________

2 'It's too hot here for a snowball!' ___________

3 'You can't make snowballs.' ___________

4 'This is fantastic!' ___________

5 'Thank you!' ___________

6 'But you can have a nice, cold drink!' ___________

Talk **Do you like this story? Talk to a friend.**

The Highest Mountain in the World

Talk **Do you know the name of the highest mountain in the world? Talk to a friend.**

1 Read about Mount Everest.

Mount Everest is the highest mountain in the world. It is 8848 meters high. Mount Everest is in Asia, and is over 60 million years old. It is very cold at the top of Mount Everest, so nothing lives there.

Talk **Do you know more about Mount Everest? Talk to a friend.**

2 **Answer the questions about Mount Everest.**

1 How high is Mount Everest?

____

2 How old is Mount Everest?

____

3 Is it hot at the top of Mount Everest?

____

4 Can anything live at the top of
Mount Everest?

____

3 **Draw a mountain. Is it a hot mountain or a cold, snowy mountain?**

Do you know about a mountain in your country? Tell a friend about the mountain.

Picture Dictionary

bottom

bus

coat

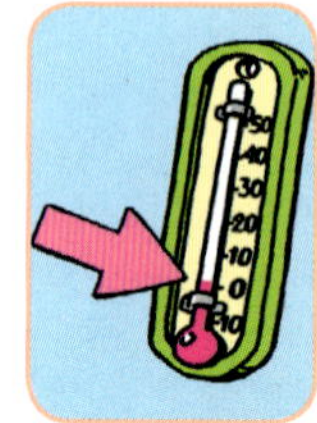

cold

down

drink

edge

hat

head

high

hot

house

lake

light

melt

mountain

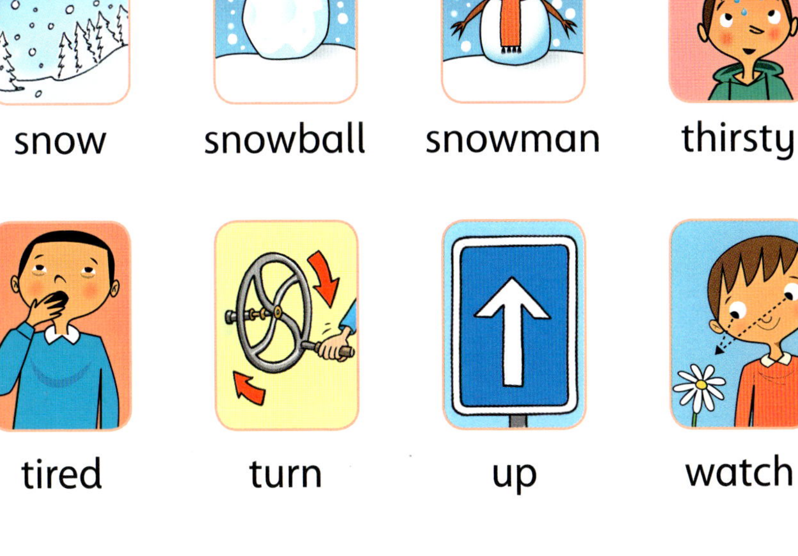

over	 path	 place	 pool
 roll	 run	 screen	 ski
 snow	 snowball	 snowman	 thirsty
tired	turn	up	watch

Oxford Read and Imagine

Oxford Read and Imagine graded readers are at nine levels (Early Starter, Starter, Beginner, and Levels 1 to 6) for students from age 3 or 4 and older. They offer great stories to read and enjoy.

Activities provide Cambridge Young Learners Exams preparation. See Key below.

At Levels 1 to 6, every storybook reader links to an **Oxford Read and Discover** non-fiction reader, giving students a chance to find out more about the world around them, and an opportunity for Content and Language Integrated Learning (CLIL).

For more information about **Read and Imagine**, and for Teacher's Notes, go to
www.oup.com/elt/teacher/readandimagine

KEY
 Activity supports Cambridge Young Learners Starters Exam preparation
 Activity supports Cambridge Young Learners Movers Exam preparation

Oxford Read and Discover

What animals live in the mountains? What plants grow there? To find out more about mountains, you can read this non-fiction book.

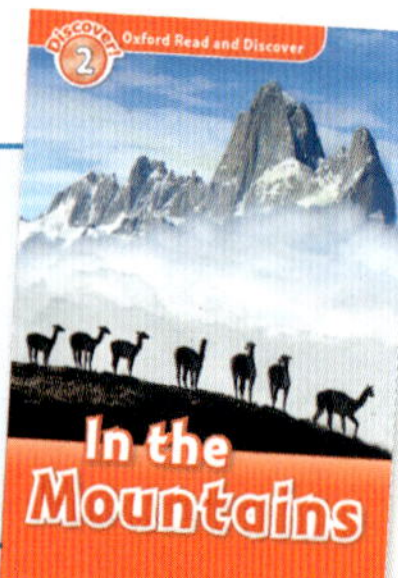

OXFORD
UNIVERSITY PRESS

Great Clarendon Street, Oxford, OX2 6DP, United Kingdom

Oxford University Press is a department of the University of Oxford. It furthers the University's objective of excellence in research, scholarship, and education by publishing worldwide. Oxford is a registered trade mark of Oxford University Press in the UK and in certain other countries

© Oxford University Press 2017

The moral rights of the author have been asserted

First published in 2017

2022

10 9 8

No unauthorized photocopying

ISBN: 978 0 19 473651 0

Printed in China

This book is printed on paper from certified and well-managed sources

ACKNOWLEDGEMENTS

Main illustrations by: Fabiano Fiorin/ Milan Illustrations Agency.

Additional illustrations by: Dusan Pavlic/ Beehive Illustration, Alan Rowe, Mark Ruffle.

The publisher would like to thank the following for permission to reproduce photographs: OUP RF p. 36 (kaetana).